Flow

flow
andrys onsman

Flow
ISBN paperback: 9781761097003
ISBN Ebook: 9781761097010
Copyright © text Andrys Onsman 2025
Cover design by Graham Davidson
Cover photo coutesy of Pexels & Anni Roenkae

First published 2025 by
Ginninderra Press
PO Box 2 Bentleigh 3204
ginninderrapress.com.au

Contents

Genealogy
- Ancestry — 9
- Nocturne — 10
- The Last Light of the Day — 11
- On Becoming Yorich — 13
- Remembrance Day — 14
- The Moral Dimension of Ancestry — 15
- Lapwing's Egg — 16
- Remembering Toscana — 17
- Ceremony — 18
- Flowering Eucalypt — 22
- The Poet's Table — 23
- Aubade — 25
- Spirit River — 26
- The Rustle in the Reeds — 27
- Well Played, Old Chap! — 28
- Ghosts of the Night Mist — 29

The Four Tasks of Creation
- The Four Tasks of Creation — 33

Improvisation
- Four Improvisations for Rob Burke — 49
- Free Music — 56
- Proprioception — 57
- Improvising Freeness — 58
- Coal Train — 60

The Rivers of North-west Tasmania
- Spanning the World — 63
- Finding Tasmania — 64
- Stealing the Island — 65

Joining the Dots	66
The Lost Rivers	67
Finding Flow	68
Crossing the Rubicon – 1	69
Crossing the Rubicon – 2	70
Crossing the Rubicon – 3	71
Crossing the Rubicon – 4	72
Muddy Creek Bridge	73
Spirit: The Mersey – 1	74
Spirit: the Mersey – 2	75
Don Heads	76
Quietly Counting Platypus	77
Reserve	78
Diluvial – the Forth River Floods	79
Cam Bridge	81
Bridging the Cam	83
To Be a Duck	85
Illumination	86
Flooding the Black River	87
The Inglis	90
The Last Yeoman of the Leven River	91
Trout Fishing on the Blythe	94
The Last Duchess	97
Wild Rivers	100
Estuarine Flow	101

Genealogy

Ancestry

The proposition in an ancestry tree presented
As a chart that identifies who begot whom,
Laid out like a skeleton in two dimensions
Is, like all unhyperlinked lists, only possibly true.

In real dimensions, an account of a life is
More like the trace of a pinball as it bounces
With unforeseen energies from unsuspected
Obstacles via disruptive barriers to a final tilt.

In real dimensions, ancestry is a wave, droplets
Of potential energised enough to stimulate new
Possibilities, chains of action to snake and ladder
Through time passing wherever there are gaps.

Ancestry is meaningless without real dimensions.
Devoid of context or perspective, a spreadsheet
Of the voiceless past lacks form and function.
And without a voice, it lacks direction and desire.

Nocturne

for Ynys Onsman

The night. A squall flings rain on the roof,
a sharp tattoo that mutes the ocean's roar,
and holds the dark, itself an endless sea.
Each window checked and made secure before
The curtain's drawn, the fire guarded now,
The glowing eyes of embers impotent.

Between a sleeping wife and bedside light
I lie awake, despite my tired eyes,
And listen as the house becomes a ship.
On nights like this, when you were cot-tied small,
You'd jolt at sudden sounds as if they were
Commands, then squirm yourself into your quilt.

The flow of time is an illusion we create
By force of will. Tomorrow is another day.

The Last Light of the Day

As often as I can, I'll fly from home to home,
To feel the coastline's sea-salt air caress my face
Even if the polders are fenced and smaller now.

The past condensed to vague vignettes, incidents that
Rest on time contested memories, unverified by anyone
Except the teller of the tale. Nothing matters now

Beyond the memories that shape a man, regardless
Of how true they are. Standing on the sleeper dyke
The memories are vague but true enough for me.

In winter when the ice was thick enough to turn
The water underneath into a silent, black portent
We lived in town, in older, less expensive streets

Cocooned in prison rooms guarded by the cold,
Until when school was done, the sun came out, the door
Was opened and we burst out like scattered shot.

It took the best part of a day to bus and then to walk
Far enough away from urban dirt to breathe the air
Of pastures ploughed, of cows released from byres.

We swapped our plastic Jesus boots for clogs and boots
And headed to the sea, to look for flowing streams to cross,
To count the bobby calves, to hunt for lapwing eggs.

The farmhouse where I lived in summer months has shrunk.
The owners drive to work each day in less than half an hour
And have no time for bobby calves or lapwing eggs or streams.

Not theirs, the eyes that see past what there is and focus on
The building blocks of memory that rearrange themselves
To suit a changing narrative. I am the teller of this tale.

On Becoming Yorich

Now too old to die too young
The past outweighs what's yet to come.
All my running ahead has slowed
To looking behind, reluctantly.
As how I see myself grows clearer
How I'm seen grows more dim.
I'll be transparent the day I die
Or vice versa, even though

Everything I have been, I still am
Regardless that it matters less and less.
The opportunities to be have grown fewer
As the might-have-beens have increased.
To feast on every fortune given me
Required a fiercer appetite than mine.
But I have swallowed all I've bitten off.

Far from infinite, my jests
Never numbered more than one.
Told with neither a whimper nor a bang
But overwhelming all that still remains.
No fool demands a legacy beyond
Acknowledgement and nothing at all
When his soul has left his skull. But
That my fancies were excellent is true.

Remembrance Day

The luck of growing old, bearing
Witness to another setting of the sun
With the expectation of its rising

Ought to be celebrated
Not only for not surviving a war
But in general, like a Lotto win.

It's easier of course, to feel
Resentment, regret, frustration
With each new perceived decline,

To see the endgame draw nearer
To feel the allotment of time grow smaller
To know the empty day is coming,

To realise that you won't be
In the lives to come, your voice unheard,
Your being static in someone's stories

That every day's a dress rehearsal
For the final show, the off-coil shuffle,
To be the one remembered

Instead of the one remembering.
I lean into my philosophy, a hope
That I will have been happy enough.

The Moral Dimension of Ancestry

The ancestors have outlived memory,
And lie wrapped up in records that survive
As hyperlinked reality and have
No agency in any search for truth.

And being dead, the ancestors ignore
The rules of moral certitude of now;
Their sins and virtues recontextualised
And made irrelevant within the here.

The ancestors, if far enough away
From us and how we live, exist beyond
The pale, that line between what's
Thought to be acceptable and what's not.

The ancestors, immune to doubt, refuse
To kneel before what's yet to come or god.

Lapwing's Egg

We were children, gumboots, shorts and overcoats
Hair whipped by North Sea winds, the taste of salt
In the air, half-dancing half-running after the men.

There were fewer fences then, less concern over who
Owned what and where we might go in search of
The first egg laid by a lapwing. Should we be the first

To find a nest, we would take one from the clutch
And if it could be verified, then one of us,
Not me for sure, would be allowed to present it

To the Queen, who'd smile and say a few words
And we'd be shy, bursting with pride, and curtsy
Or bow in borrowed clothes, be stunned by the flash.

Of course, it never was us, or anyone like us whose
Photograph adorned the news. The children who
Presented a speckled green egg to Her Majesty

Were tidy, hair crisply parted, pullovers and pants
And fathers in suits and mothers with permanent hair,
Beaming with confidence and well-maintained teeth.

None of that mattered as we bounded like puppies
In the wake of our father and uncle, men who knew
Where the lapwings made nests, men without suits.

Our place wasn't in palaces or front pages of papers.
We knew our place. The meadows behind the sea-dyke
Were our home. We'd never run freely anywhere else.

Remembering Toscana

For Hazel Flynn

How time writes on white paper wings. It seems
An age ago that we were speeding down
Patrician roads, Italian driveways that
Promised nothing more than shouted dead ends.
You did your level best to keep the peace but

But backseats never have the final word.
I was at the wheel, uncertain, then as now,
Right until the villa broke through the mist
That shields all magic lakes and dreamtime myths.
Having exhausted the drive, we exhaled,
Delivered our bags to the dust of our digs
And walked to the bar to revive and restore.
You toasted the trip with a glass of red wine.

High in Toscana, as we sat, backs to the wall,
And drank in the last rays of sun on the hills, a
Zephyr blew, a gentle caress of the skin,
Each one of us silent, a moment at peace,
Listening to us as we listened to it.

Ceremony

1

Despite our reluctance for sanctified mourning
We came to the funeral of my father's friend.
A mirror pair of immigrants, old countrymen,
They'd shared the burden of their ferpleatsing.

In the church, there without conviction, cold
On the wooden pew, formally quiet, dressed
uncomfortably on a Friday in our Sunday best
I sat next to my father white bearded, tired, old.

This man who was my strength and heart,
My confidence, my recklessness and fear,
My start, progenitor of all of us out here,
Less foreign than him, a grafted part

The man who could never fade or grow dim
Like a shadow to the past, forgotten bits,
unconnected memories, random hits
This man next to me, everything in him

Was disappearing. Without thinking he took
My hand, as I had taken his to allay the fears
Of growing older, losing love, bitter tears
Cried over separations, the thrown book,

The hand of a man who had been so strong
Now in need of mine, all of my grateful heart
In my fingers, wrapped around each part
Of him, each muscle, each fight, each song.

He was recognisably there, gone somehow
But still alive within me, on a foreign pew
Seeing off a vestiged life, unhappy with this new
version of himself, friendless and old now.

He'd never knelt for God, for France or Rome.
During the meaningless words for the dead,
My father leaned in, an intimate move, and said
'When I have died, don't do this. Bring me home.'

II

Back home, on the sleeper dike,* the wind
Refused to ease, dusk made darker by a sky
Full of clouds that threatened to rain and I
Wondered if this was what he'd had in mind

When he imagined his return to it heitelân.
All that was left of him in a grey plastic urn,
Checked-in luggage, was coffin wood burned
To ashes, to be scattered here, finally gone.

There was nothing tangible, no spirit or spark,
No ceremonial patterns, no text or funeral guide
For the cluster of the waiting kin, standing outside
In the wind, the rain, wary of the growing dark.

Nothing else to do then, but throw him in the air
Before all light has faded. I turned my back,
And laughed at the silliness of this final act,
Ashes on my face, the old man still in my hair.

A ceremony, genuinely felt but so absurd,
A fitting end to a maelstrom of a life. The rain
Made good its threat, we headed home again
Laughing that weather should be his final word

And brought back the man he'd been instead
Of the one he'd drifted into. He could still evince
A sympathetic smile and I could tell him that since
I'd brought him home, he'd never could be dead.

Ferpleatsing – displacement, exile
It Heitelân – literally 'The Fatherland', that is, Fryslân
The saying 'Frisians only kneel before God' refers to their refusal to kneel before Charlemagne. It may well be a myth but the idea of freedom remains dear to the Frisians.
* A sleeper dike is a back-up to the sea dike. It is rarely touched by seawater.

Flowering Eucalypt

Executing the terms of my mother's will
Required permission from the old farm's
New owners to plant a tree by the side of the dam

Because dying didn't dampen her desire
To drive roots into the land she'd adopted
Even though it had always stayed wary of her.

Surviving the thromboses that were drifting
Deep in her veins for just long enough
To hold her long longed-for first grandchild,

A harbinger of the half dozen yet to come,
And having ticked the migrant mother boxes,
Education, employment, a suitable match

And a link to the old world while embracing
The new, there was no time left for herself,
No time to rest her factory feet and dream,

No time to be recognised outside her family,
All of them gone, empty house echoes, no time
To search and to find her young self in her art.

Allowed unchecked passage, the clots chained,
Empoldered a beachhead that expanded until
It dammed the flow of blood to her heart,

Her ambitions made real by the flowers that bloom
On the multiple branches of the eucalyptus that,
Fed by her ashes, grows tall by the side of the dam.

The Poet's Table

for Stephen Edgar

We were sat at the poet's table
In his house on the hill in the Glebe.
I'd shown you some lines, not yet a poem
And you, still to be burdened by acclaim,
Though Queueing For the Mud Club
Was about to afford you your due,
Read the piece with unwarranted care
And found something productive to say.

Of course, you would. It was you. Every
Word has to work, each sentence a base
For the next, nudging the reader to see
The unseen that was there all along
And be moved by the sight.

I mistook your kindness for praise
And after scant revision submitted the poem,
Then waited, and with each passing day
Lost heart, (I was younger, thinner-skinned)
Until it was published and I saw it in print,
Near the back, with my name misspelled
But recognisably mine.

Fifty years on, my name on spines,
I found it by chance and actually cringed
At its artifice, then laughed at myself and
Remembered with fondness the man
Who'd sat for an hour or more

With me at the table of our mutual friend.
You'll not remember that day, why should you?
Just one of many, and so much ahead that
An inept pastiche about a cave-dwelling bat
From a unvetted acquaintance could be
Of no significance to you

But to me that day was a watershed
And I am just as grateful now as then.

Aubade

for Anne Wilks

Behind the useless blackout drapes, the sun
Insists the working day has now begun
Despite the counterargument that night
Is measured by the hours slept, not by light
Delivered far too soon and far too bright
And smugly careless of the needs of anyone
Who drank the night until the wine had gone
As we, too old for such a thing, had done.

Awake, we stay cocooned in bed despite
The need to wee, and curse this appetite
For wanton self-destruction dressed as fun,
To strip back layers like a fleece unspun.
We move to touch, enjoy this prize we won
By simply being here. We reunite.

Spirit River

for Jan Onsman

The rivers of my empoldered childhood
Are the lines that box in Mondriaan's swatches
Of colour, ordered, flat, made by man not God
And therefore thought to be unworthy of remark.

I have a photo, grainy black and white, me small,
Sitting with my father as he fishes in the ditch between
The meadows, the vast expanse of channelled green,
Bovine trampled, mud mixed with shit in the rain,

Me, blond and much too small for such horizons,
Leaning into his pitch black coat, warmed by his being
There, in that moment, with me, intent on watching
The upward pointing dobber, shifting to accommodate me,

And in the line of that straight canal, that soulless flow
Sliding like lead in its cold narrow ditch, a spirit runs
As wild as any made by god, if god is the sum of all
That's been created by anything but man.

The Rustle in the Reeds

for Baukje Wytsma

Every day is settled in its place and past.
The folk who work within the cadences
of this verdant land, listen to the birds,
the shifting wind and breaking sea, and
the whispers in the branches of the trees.
In damp clothes smelling of earth and rain,
With fingers stiffened by frost, leather-faced
and dreaming, they mind their business.

The need to work is chiseled into life,
the patterns set in stone. Every day, they
push, feeling, gauging, judging, into the herd,
or plough another furrow, plant another crop
with hope, and pass by with a nod, a brief hello,
a finger raised to touch a cap, folk who keep
the rustle in the reeds to themselves.

It is the way it's always been, unrelenting. Because
I'm born to it, the rhythm, of this lived-in landscape,
manufactured and renewed, is my pulse. I dance
around the corpse-wain like a bride enchained,
always drawn towards the rustle in the reeds.

Well Played, Old Chap!
on reaching 50

Halfway there, the score acknowledged with
A nod to the folk who've come to watch you
Play, to enjoy the sound of leather on wood and
Pay attention to the rise and fall, applaud as
You negotiate the innings into deeper water.

Between deliveries you might look up to see
If all those who promised to be there, are
Responding to the moves you're making,
The reaching cover drives, the body swerves,
Happy to see you survive another swinging ball
Delivered at a fearsome pace from far too close
And smile as you dance around the spinning ones.
Your defence is sound, your attack is sure.

So, enjoy the acclaim, the warm applause,
The cheers for what's achieved so far, not
Easily attained but earned. Take a moment to
Validate what's been achieved up to this point.
Each run is valuable, a base necessity, another

Piece of the puzzle put in place. Enjoy the
Accolades that will flow your way this day.
In the words of that old Persian poet
Xenophon, 'The sweetest sound is praise.'

Ghosts of the Night Mist

Truganini to Gwen Harwood

I'm asking you to shift the time from then
to now because you're good at sleight of hand,
creating masks and other worlds with which

to cloak yourself. Your voice, at every turn
bespoke, can sing with truth, as light as tears
at night, as cruel as death before its time.

I dare to ask because we share so much:
The weight of exile heavy on our backs,
The water, height, the pain, the need to lie,

And how I envy your ability to get back
More than you would give away, to control.
They ripped mine out without consent.

You wrote me out before, believed the lies
Without a thought but now you have a chance
To make amends. You owe me that at least.

Reluctant icons of the modern age,
Our image made to fit the narrative
But I'm no longer asked to say a word

We're both of us a catch, dead fish on land
A palimpsest beneath the pressing weight
Of monument, of scholarship, of dust

Behind a veil of scattered ash and words
A murmurating, spindled universe
In which we'll play no part. We'll disappear

Unless you speak before we lose our voice,
Before we are erased, before we fall,
Before we're reconciled into the past.

The Four Tasks of Creation

The Four Tasks of Creation

Psyche, a beautiful young woman without a hint of guile or artifice, spurns all advances from mortals and gods alike until Eros, sent by his jealous mother Aphrodite to make her fall in love with someone ugly and old and thereby stop being a threat to her own status as the most beautiful female, falls in love with her himself. Because she is a mortal and he is a god they agree to keep his identity secret, even from her, and only meet at night, in darkness.

While Psyche is quite happy with the arrangement, her unkind, less beautiful sisters convince her to light a candle and make sure that he isn't some sort of monster. She does, sees he is beautiful but before she can extinguish the flame, a drop of wax falls on him and he wakes. Furious at her betrayal of trust, he flees back to his mother and refuses to talk to her, a situation wholly welcomed by Aphrodite.

Distraught at losing the love of her life, she asks his mother what she needs to do to be allowed to talk to him. Aphrodite sets her four tasks – each of which is seemingly impossible. The first task is to sort in one night a giant heap of jumbled seeds into separate piles. The second is to gather some of the Golden Fleece. The third is to fill a crystal flask with water from the River Styx. The fourth is to descend into Hell and fill a box with Persephone's secret beauty cream.

Against all odds and with an occasional helping hand, Psyche completes all the task, convincing Eros of her commitment and he frees himself from his mother's shackles and marries Psyche. To avoid complications, Zeus turns Psyche into a god and she and Eros with their daughter Hedone, live happily on Olympus, forgotten until psychoanalysis appropriates their names.

Prologue

Some say the fin de siècle Viennese
Did nothing more than simply name
The syndromes, the state of minds
Disturbed and shaken by dis-ease,

Complexes that are angel-kissed,
Memories of the traumatic kinds,
Repression of anger, joy and pain,
Conditions that did not exist

Until they were identified
By students of behaviour keen
To be the first to allocate a label
To any variation of the norm,

Like wild desire that won't conform,
Or anything that might be seen
As strange, odd or a touch unstable
To be examined and then classified.

They took the name of any god who
Populated ancient panoplies
And dragged it down to archetype
Or id, interpretations on the whole

Constructed without proof, just to
Make their psychoanalyses
Sound plausible. Ignore the hype.
Before we had a mind, we had a soul.

1 Separating Seeds

Let's park impracticalities
And start by asking why.
Oh, I know your mind has turned
To sex and procreation or
To racial purity, but neither
Seems enough for this command.
I think this is about ideas.

The metaphor of choice that
Ideas begin as seeds is so ingrained
That even though an MRI
Will show ideas are neurons
Connecting, finding a path
Not previously taken, which is
A metaphor itself, it still remains.

Be that as it may, the point
Is that ideas need to be sorted out.
Sure, let your mind go where it will
But that going is a line of thought,
A neural network, or if you need
The comfort of familiar words,
The germination of a seed.

Therefore, Psyche on her knees and
Weeping at the magnitude of this,
Her first assignment, or hurdle if you will,
Is for her to get her head together,
Tidy up her thinking, and nothing
Is better at cleaning house than

An army of ants, robotic and precise,
The mechanism that the mind
Will use to recalibrate itself
when given half a chance.
In the morning, the night's despair
Is clarified, the end in sight
And you're ready to resume.

Creative ideation is unjumbling
The confusion of imbroglios,
Allowing seeds set in familiar soil
To be cross-fertilised relationships
And blossom without overthinking
From an agitated mind. Ideation
Is allowing ants to do their work.

2 Gathering the Golden Fleece

When I was young
I wondered what the Golden Fleece
Could have to do with petrol pumps.
At school I learned that sheep
Were metaphors for wealth,
The country rode upon their backs
Into a new prosperity.

A migrant child
Too young and filled with fear to speak
I kept my tales inside my head
Where Jason and his Argonauts could sail
Without the need for foreign words
Or explanations too obscure for
The new Australian psyche.

That eastern folk
Used the fleece of sheep to pan for gold
Was interesting but not enough
To dull the power of the myths.
The Golden Fleece was safe
From being washed away
With other childhood things.

The best ideas
Will hang around. Or slip away
And then return to plug a gap
You hadn't known was there.
When sent to fetch a skein of wool
From rutting rams, it's best to improvise,
Approach it from the side.

Allow the thorns
To do the work. Randy rams have
Itchy skin that a bristly bush relieves.
They'll scratch themselves, leave
Bits of fleece fluttering in the breeze.
When they've done their thing and left,
You hold your nose, collect.

3 Sampling the River Styx

It goes against the grain, the River Styx.
Because it flows uphill
It is, of course, the liars' paradox,

The borderline between this world and Hell
A one-way gate with locks
Impossible to pick and never still.

The river's curse is honesty and truth.
The water dulls your power
to obfuscate, create a shibboleth,

To make believe you are an honest liar
Although all truth is myth
Including truth that's buried in desire,

The wanting something more than life can give,
The recklessness of love,
The need to find another path, to live

Outside the comfort and the safety of
The impulse to forgive
Yourself, to rest on merely good enough.

The best advice is not to contemplate
The stream. Stay well away,
No one should be made to be so brave

At someone else's bidding. Anyway,
The choices that you made
Before you saw the light are chains today.

But if you should still want to fill that flask
You must come well-prepared
Because there are no guides, no one to ask,

The water's maelstrom-wild, the banks too hard
To clamber down, the task
Impossible for anyone not scared

Enough for sheer adrenalin, with speed
And fear to cast all doubt
Aside, forget the danger, and proceed

With no regard to reason, all stops out.
In order to succeed
Don't doubt yourself, be crazy-brave throughout,

Beyond all fear and reason. Bear in mind
The stupid reason why
You broke a promise of the sacred kind.

Because your sisters ordered, you complied
While knowing love is blind
And that the heart's more honest than the eye.

Had you refused, ignored them out of hand
Declined to play along
With them and drawn a border in the sand,

You would have learnt your heart was strong
Enough and can withstand
The pressure of the jealous sirens' song.

Your weeping now is purposeless. To doubt
Is failing before its done.
To fear is to anticipate without

Desire. Take this chance before it's gone
Before the flame goes out.
The seed's been sown, the golden fleece is spun.

The river is another step along the path
Towards the stronger you,
The one who doesn't fear the aftermath

Of taking unplanned chances. Nothing true
Has ever come to pass
Without a reckless leap into the new.

4 Persephone's Box

Remember how your hands were
Shaking, when we met in Hell?
Were you exhausted, afraid
or simply cold? Perhaps all three.

In any case, you were spent
And overwrought, shivering on
The point of collapse, but here
You were, pleading for my balm.

Your gown was torn, the vent
You slipped down was narrow,
The rocky edges sharp and cruel
As shafts into underworld must be.

Like a homeless refugee, the coins
You gave the ferryman, the cost
Of visiting the dead, was all your wealth.
Well sister, nothing comes for free.

And perhaps you should have kept
The cakes you fed the black-souled dog
In case your mission fell apart
And you had need of them yourself.

Every pleading voice you heard
Was hers or yours, his or everyone's
But your resolve was wax in your ears,
Because you cannot save the world.

You've done all that but not enough
For now you're begging me and why
Should I fill your cask with balm
When that is all I have to bargain with?

Look up, sister, and listen now to me
For although everything I've said is true
There is much that's still unsaid. I have
A proposition that benefits us both.

Any fool can see how this will end
You are bound to be a god yourself
We all are gods within ourselves
Of course, that's very likely true

But you, my love, are destined to
Live within the gods, an inner beauty
Without guile that makes my salve
A superficial wax, skin-deep at best.

Once you're deified, you'll need
To understand your enemies
And keep an eye on friends, for one
Will be the other and sometimes both.

Be forewarned, my sweet, that gods
Are inconsistent and unkind
Dispensing favours among themselves
With precious little thought or fear.

You know that every heaven is
Constructed as it needs to be
At any given time, from wishes
And vague expedient lies.

Every one of us is someone's whim
Or fancy, nightmare or defence.
We are more ethereal than hope
And less robust than those who dream.

Let us, my heart, then make a pact
A secret, sacred tryst to watch
Each other's back, for ever to protect
Ourselves from exploitation and denial.

Here's my proposition, sworn between
Just you and me. I'll fill your empty box
With balm if you give me, without
Pretence, your genuine embrace.

Knowing that this bargain is the casket
You must never open, never use to seek
Revenge, never turn into a dagger, and
Never tell a soul. But never forget.

Epilogue – Hedonism

The need to make a joyous, vibrant thing
Is not complex, despite the contrary view
Espoused by psychoanalysis. To bring
Ideas into the world, create a new
Exciting work that elevates the heart
Beyond the here and now is not divine
But human. Nothing's more mundane than art.
Its meaningless insistence underlines
Our little worlds. We think, we love, we feel,
Enjoy our days. We only wish for more
If the time we had to live was spent without
Reward or in denial, preparing for
An after-life of sorts, a place not real
Unless it's made before the lights go out.

Improvisation

Four Improvisations for Rob Burke

1

To start with nothing,
No more than a compulsive
Need to make a thing
That won't exist until
It has been made and
If it isn't done, will
Never exist at all,

Like love unfelt. If love's
Not felt it can't exist and if
It can't exist, it won't be felt.

Like caged animals, birds
Jaguars and pacing tigers
I wonder if love no longer
Felt still exists. I wonder because
It still radiates from me unasked.
I have no choice but give
The love that only you could feel
Even though you, long gone,
No longer can feel a thing.

This is how we build a life
Big enough to hold ourselves
And others who we need to feel
In the building of it.
We improvise until
The world exists
And we have nothing more
To add to it.

2

The effort to distort the sound
That barges from his saxophone
Screws up his body, stance and face
As much as it does the music itself.

But more to the point,
The sound he makes distorts the truth,
Not by lying to evade or impress
But by offering something wild,
Beyond the pale, not yet set,
Another version of the story, a
Moving of parameters of what is
And what is understood to be true.

It's easier to dismiss this as not
Being music, to judge it just noise,
as if being just is somehow a crime
but you can skate on very thin ice
as long as it is just thick enough
and your skill at skating matches
what is needed to fly.

No words
Or images exist beyond the solid state,
The electronic honesty of noiseless bias
Or bias without any noise. Distortion
Replaces the dirt of the road less travelled
That commodification has wiped clean.
Truth will always be distorted but
Distortion will sometimes be true.

You can slide without slipping away.

3

Writing a new poem
Is playing free music
With rhythm and feel
And harmonics enough
To let it find its way.

You step into the spotlight
In a shadowed-filled room,
A round of applause
To heighten expectation
To make something happen,

And you improvise
Testing ideas to see
If they fit into something
That doesn't exist until
It's obvious and there.

So how do you know
If what you're saying will
Fit into what you've already said?
How can you tell
If the story is true?

You might wait for echoes,
Replies to the questions,
Respond to new points of view
See if the flow will take you
Beyond the here and now.

You make marks and play
Until you're in the music
And the music is living in you
And all you can do is add
To the poem that's there.

4

'And that was every cliché in the book,'
You said as if it were a crime but what
Did you expect? You called a Bb blues
And signalled changes with a leading look
Demanding total freedom to explore
Your own ideas regardless how obtuse
They may appear to be to us who sit

Off stage in darkness, shadows still as stone,
Our knowledge of the theory much too scant
To understand the brave new harmonies
The reinvented sonic paths, the tone
Of stolen Afrologic melodies
To listen, happy to be ignorant,
And take our comfort in the joy of it.

Free Music

When the noise in my head
Morphs into music
I wish I could plug you
Into my brain.

The sound of the notes
That commit to the flow
Of the song is complete
And enough in itself.

So, if you see me smiling
When there's nothing to see
I'm probably listening
And might even dance.

Proprioception

for Rafferty Needham

We've given names to rhythms we can feel,
A march, a waltz, or rock and roll, just count
It in and off we go. We jump into
The flow, our cells react without command
To pulsing noise, to rhythms felt, to beat
Without a conscious thought we are aware
Of how our bodies move and where we are
In space. Alive, directionless and free,

I watch you dance, the way you show no fear,
Intent, the way you let your body be
Alive, as if you're thinking on your feet,
As if the here and now is all that's real,
As if ambition overcomes what's planned,
As if the need for safe will disappear.

Improvising Freeness
for Raymond MacDonald

To begin again where I left off,
Somewhere in the middle eight
Of a not yet finished answer to
A question about the construction

Of real but unrealised potential
Hidden in the path of time passing.
It's always far too fucking serious
When it's your arse that's dragging.

Anyway, I'll go on building up
This thing, now that it's been started
Because a book unwritten can't be read
Which is as serious as you can make it.

The rules don't apply. I don't count
Nor do I know the tune but at least
I don't have to explain what I do
To anyone and in that way I'm free

To wander over the topography
Inside my head, regardless of the world
Outside, except where it intrudes
In ways that are too fucking serious

Or, if you're in luck, in ways that are
Sharp enough to make you laugh or cry,
Or be awed by the intrusion and you see
It as a bridge to somewhere new.

This construct, existing as it's built,
Stretches out like a cat on death row,
Moved from box to gallows with a glance
And, when it swings, released and free.

Coal Train

The sound that unravels
The thread of fashion,
Tears time apart without
A beg your pardon,
Without excuse, without a name,
Without regret or explanation.
Listen before it gets caught by
Review and opinion,
Before it gets indexed by,
Genre and style,
Before it sinks into
Theory, before it is
Stored and contained,
Made to fit into
Retrospect by nothing
That it was when
It was wild,
The sound that
Even when it's
Recognised,
Theorised,
Cauterised
By ism or ology,
Never fails to
Flow

The Rivers of North-west Tasmania

Spanning the World

We live connected, be it through the links of
Of cells in us or through the us in cells.
To make what's all around us real, we first
Must make the world anew each day from bits
And bobs, a make-do edifice from all
That's known. The present world is my best guess
And history a file of old mistakes
To which I'll add today when it is done.
We'll peek into another's world to look
For common ground, to see if they agree
With how we see the world, for truth is true
When everyone agrees. With fingers crossed
The world is built to span the gaps between
What's been, what is and what is yet to come.

Finding Tasmania

They sailed on God's command to shine a light
Onto the lesser, hidden world, and so
The island, once a world within itself,
Became a new frontier in need of links
And ownership. To prove the point, they raised
A Union Jack while blind to inland hues.
The purple, brown and green outlined in black
Remains an unrecognised palimpsest.
The natural world scraped clean, the soil prepared,
Ambitions primed, imaginations roused,
The owning by naming, the periplus logs,
The maps and the charts, the surveys and grants,
The plans unreal until a deed in hand,
says this what isn't mine to give is yours.

Stealing the Island

At first, the settlers staked their claims into
The ground around the rivers' open mouths.
Forever yearning to be going home,
They kept their backs towards the island's heart.
The inland was a foreign land, too dark
Too dense to penetrate, regardless of the fact
Of pre-existing walking trails that ran
Through managed land, of pre-existing life,
As if some unimportant bits and bobs
Remain too far beyond the bridges' span.
The irony of Scottish names for peaks
And rivers unexplored and not yet cleared
Escaped the atlas maker's eye. Perhaps
It was a warning to prepare for graft.

Joining the Dots

The rivers ran like spirits, free and fast
Unwilling to be crossed. A river needs
An age to scratch itself into the rocks.
The time it takes to find its soul is set
In stone. A river makes itself anew
Each day but so do we, albeit not
The same. Depending on our point of view
It separates us from each other or
It borders our domains. It matters not.
The rivers writhe like dragons, but
All to no avail. The settlers brought their world
Of links and spans, their need for joining dots
And making chains, connecting cells until
Each claim was truth and every river crossed.

The Lost Rivers

Where once we sailed from place to place by sea
We now could circumnavigate the isle
By road and in a hundred years we made
Each river town the same. A bridge conveys
The common concepts of community,
A world contained within the here and now.
Comparison breeds competition based
On fear of missing out; entitlement
Created by the unseen hand of God
If God is advertising undreamt dreams
And manifests in local council rooms.
From Port Sorell to Circular Head, each town
Demands to be the same. If Burnie has
A cycle path, then Wynyard needs one too.

Finding Flow

The rivers run with broken flows but still
They run. The arrogance to think the dams
And weirs, the fords and bridges are enough
To break a spirit. Do we think that wharves
And docks, that water views and lawns have made
The rivers ours? That we are in control
Beyond the instant of the here and now?
The truth is we can make as many worlds
As fit into philosophy but none
Will last for ever, none will satisfy
The bits and bobs, the cells in us, the us
In cells, the need to span a gap. In truth,`
Beyond the flow, beyond the here and now,
Beyond the word, a river has no need of us.

Crossing the Rubicon – 1

When Caesar crossed Rubicon there was
No turning back. The man he'd been was left
Behind, a sloughed-off skin discarded like
A wasted dream, unspoken and foregone.

A robust man, he'd tied his fate to gods
Who ruled within the lesser pantheon,
Concerned with luck, the need to stay alive
Or failing that, to grant a decent death.

No epithet is carved in stone. Our bones
Return to dust and reputations fall
To doubt when misremembered deeds
Are changed to fit a later narrative.

Once crossed, there is no point in looking back:
With luck, the plaudits earned will stay alive.

Crossing the Rubicon – 2

And what about the ones who stay behind?
The timid ones, unsure and circumspect,
Applaud those sure of heart who ford the stream,
Then turn and go about their usual day.

They also count who stand and wait, who watch
The others cross, who turn, reverse and choose
To stay, forego the final push into
The great unknown, who see no need to chance

Our arm, uncertain of the sacrifice.
We ask, with due regard, what Caesar wants
And whose renown we're meant to write. The choice
Is ours or else it is no choice. We know

We serve our gods, deny ourselves although
We too have lines to etch in stone. We live.

Crossing the Rubicon – 3

Like bedside Fates, her daughters gathered near
To watch her passing to the other side.
No statement of intent had crossed her lips
The process took its cue from other signs.

Well past the span of three score years and ten,
The royal telegram within her sight
A well-played innings closed without the need
To raise the bat. There was no turning back.

The nursing home is dark. The light inside
The room is soft, what's left behind's a veil,
A well-constructed web, a coat to wrap
Around herself, a comfort in the end,

Her girls, all here, their future's now her past
And even if she could, she won't look back.

Crossing the Rubicon – 4

Her death proscribed by circumstance, within
Herself she lived a different life. Her dreams
Enveiled and seldom given air, she spread
Herself among her girls, gave each a part

Of who she was, a fan of channels and she
Herself an upstream name, the Rubicon
Before it dissipates into a bay
So wide the river's gone except as what

It was. A river like a life, is past,
A record of encounters mapped in time,
Each a different view, a vague concord
Reluctant, shifting, subject to review,

A flow in space, mosaic memories that move
the splintered light into a single stream.

Muddy Creek Bridge

The tidal flats at Muddy Creek roll like the barrels
Of a well-oiled shotgun, ready to fire into the sea.
Nothing escapes in the air overhead, a filigreed sky,
A network of passages that tunnel the flow.

The old bridge was a mockery. Like a Cape Barren Goose
Uncertain on land and ungainly in flight, it swayed
And made dancers of us all, the rhythm pre-set by
The wind and the water and the wanting to cross

Over the past and uncovered ripples of mud.
The new one, accident-proof, concrete and steel
Spans over tidal flow and short circuits the time
It takes weekend cyclists to ride to the café.

Humourless and high enough to withstand any
More floods, its permanence anchored into the banks
With bolts drilled deep in bedrock. If not for the wind
And smell of the sea, you could cross with your eyes shut.

The ramshackle jetties stop short of the water and
The boats lie like beetles on the estuarine mud, masts
At an angle and ribcage exposed. The new bridge
Is a viewing deck, the old one was a part of the view.

Spirit: The Mersey – 1

It starts, as so much does, with a waterfall.
Cold water, snow barely wet, washes clean,
Tumbles over ledges, and cascades over stone,
Hidden by ferns and the mottled light of
The highlands in the heart of the island.
It bustles its way through gorges gauged
Through rock too old to be guarded by time
A testimony to perseverance and patience,
All rivers are old and everything old is a river.

No god made these canyons, there is no design.
Its spirit comes from having been and being now.
Every river is a flow, a course hewn from a single
Point of release, a Pollock petroglyph across
Immovable rock, exploiting cracks and fissures,
Caressing, soft fingers, gradually building strength
Enough to be brutal, to batter, to not care about
Aesthetics, about what we might think. What use
Might a river have of a deity? The reverse is true!

But after the event, nothing so spectacular
So biblical, so far beyond the ken of humankind
In terms of manufacture could be allowed to stay
Undeified, and so the gods were given pride of place.
The Dreaming which assigned no rank but made the world
A cornucopia of natural grace, fashioned the river
As a sacred cloak, later to be overridden by
A vengeful God demanding obeisance and fear.

Spirit: the Mersey – 2

In phone-box bright colours, giant ferries dwarf the banks,
Red for people, white for cargo and blue for cement,
Each bigger than an office block, the river barely wide
Enough to accommodate its bulk, behind the silos,
The rows of ugly concrete sentinels, a testament to
Careless commerce, they are nudged into place on
The eastern, less lovely side of the town by tugs,
Slow-motion cattle dogs that push and prod until
The behemoths are safely docked.

The estuary
Fans out like a skirt that swirls around a dancer's legs
But underneath the channel is no wider than a street.

Don Heads

Having been made to work and earn its keep
Upstream, this is the river here, a dowager
That glides away, retired and restrained,
Out to sea, dissolving into the common soul.

But walk with the river a while, through tea tree
And swaying gums, the fallen boughs that habitat
The near-forgotten birds, the whirr of wings,
The blackened heart of sassafras, the sclerophyll,
A resting snake, languid as it waves away,
The dappled light that dances with the dragonflies,
The smell of salt, the brush of leaves, there until
You reach the orange lichen covered rocks
That guard the river's mouth. Between the Heads
The river slides across the sand and twirls her skirt
Revealing a glimpse of what you'll miss as you stand
On the shore.

High on the headland, sea eagles eye the fisherfolk
Who are tied to the water with thin nylon lines, not
Bothering to launch unless they see silver hauled
Up from the sea. In the air, they circle adrift until
They tuck in their wings and streamlined and lethal,
Dive head-first into the water, emerge with a fish
Still twisting and wet in their talons, like a prize.

Quietly Counting Platypus

Under the skin of the quiet river,
Oily-furred platypuses, paddling like dogs
Unsure of their business, squirm their way
Along the banks of the lesser-known Don,
Poking their bills into sand and loose pebbles,
searching for food. A spare parts creation,
A bizarre aberration, an insult to God
And intelligent design, they clamber like beavers
out of the water to shit on dry land.

We stand on the footbridge to keep tally
And track, alert to the discounting white tail
Of a duck-diving water mouse that shares the dusk,
Much the same size and leaving a target
Of concentric rings with a similar splash.
Rakalis are bellicose, unlovable, rank
And there's no place for rats on anyone's coins.

Reserve

In Don Reserve a tawny frogmouth owl
Has hatched her eggs to great relief. A clutch
Of twitchers watched and willed the young to live.
She used the nest where last year's eggs were lost
To gusting winds, disease or feral cats,
A well-branched pine, nearby the swimming pool,
Where light through leaves provided camouflage,
A little way along the track between the creek
And where the new estate is being built
Into the corridor of native bush
Now nearly overrun by onion weed
And plastic bags. Goannas rustle in
The ferny undergrowth and wait for breaks
In traffic on the path to sun themselves.

Diluvial – the Forth River Floods

That Saturday night it rained too hard for far too long.
For folk who left their cattle on low-lying land, the tattoo
on the tin roofs, too much for the gutters, was far too loud.

At Wilmot Junction the Forth River ran eight meters,
Higher than the gates of Dante's Hell they say, and
In a night darker than a deeply buried dream, fences

Ripped from their posts, were tangled up catchalls,
Trawling nets that caught everything and rammed
It down a chute much too small. Fertile floodplains,

The river's domain long before a human gaze, careless
Of measurement and allocation, disappeared under water,
Disregarding petty surveyor pegs, scraped everything clean

From surface encampments and foreign species of plants.
The pub, near the bridge, left dirtied and bruised by
Water that elbowed past at window height, offered no refuge.

After two days, the last shreds of manicure and industry
Were caught in the diluvium that sluiced and blossomed
Into dark brown clouds far out to sea, then it stopped.

Afterwards, when the river had made its point,
It squeezed itself back into its corseted banks, demure
like a courtesan who was thought to be compliant.

Now her coquettish smile is something to be wary of.
No one will carelessly turn their back on her again,
No one will take her for granted. Not for a while.

Those who had no fallback, no recompense, shook their heads
And walked away, conceding defeat, but most who were drenched
Dried their eyes, and began to rebuild, restock, and replant.

More than a single line marking a flow, a river is never a deal.
Now, as it gurgles under the bridge and drifts languidly out
To the sea, the mudflat reeds still tremble with fear.

Cam Bridge

Cambridge, they say, is near to Heaven
A joyous asylum for the pure of thought
And penitent pilgrims seeking redemption
In towering cloisters of stone

I wouldn't know whether or not it's true.
I've never been but I like the idea of a river
Named after the bridge that crosses it
Rather than the other way around.

The bridge came first. Known by locals as
De Granta Brygge, 'the bridge across the river',
It was the pathway to the fens and worlds beyond,
A place to stop and chat a while.

When the interval between the coming and going
Lasted long enough to settle, the bridge became
A destination in itself, a place in which to dream,
Aspire and to sanctify what's dreamt

And when the sceptred isle was civilised again
This time by the haut couture of Viking French,
Cantebrigge was too earthy for the conquerors
And Cambridge wiped it clean

What else could the Cambridge cross except the River Cam?
A place to punt, to drift past spires, scatter ducks
Ideas that float beneath the willow trees, a waterway
Forever dappled, manicured and green,

Befitting an asylum for the unrepentant rich,
The sponsored learned few, and pilgrims for who
Heaven is an academic exercise way beyond
The reach of an average bridge.

Bridging the Cam

On the northwest coast of Tasmania
The new bridge that will span the River Cam,
Has no name beyond 'The Fucking Bridge'
Instead it has a timeframe and a price.
They say it will cost us twenty mil
But we all know that it will be at least
Twice that much, take twice as long to build
And bear in mind that this will be
The third time that the river's crossed.
They say the one that's there no longer serves
The highway's needs but that seems
Marginal at best, and since when do highways
Get to say what's needed on the Coast?
I've lived in Somerset for all my life
And I hadn't seen a pollie here till that joker
With the smarmy smile and Staffy eyes,
Stood underneath the overpass to tell us that
The project will increase the traffic flow
And I thought 'Fuck me dead! Who wants
More trucks come roaring through the town?'
What's more, he never said how many local kids,
The ones who cook their brains with drugs
Until they're so fucked up they kill themselves
Or play in traffic or get stabbed, who of them will get
A job or learn a trade or get a chance to grow?

I remember when the trains still ran along the coast
When the ships sailed in and out of ports, loaded high
With stuff we made, with stuff we grew, with hope.
It was another useless politician who announced
The ferry boats would stop, we'd build a wider road,
And rip away the railway line to make a cycle path.
And look how that turned out. A clutch of blokes
In nylon clothes, once a week unless it rains,
pedal to the coffee shop on flash new racing wheels.
The bridge will have a path beneath the carriageway
For pedestrians and bikes. Twenty mil! Just give us each
A half a mil and we'll swim across the Cam.

To Be a Duck

An ugly duckling turning into
A swan is occasion for fable,
The stuff of fancy, wishful envy
For most grow up to be a duck.

We swear that beauty is in the eye
Of the beholder but having a face only
A mother could love requires surgical
Intervention rather than hope.

When beauty becomes comparative
Superlative is bound to follow
Regardless of how ridiculous, the
Point and perspective will be gone.

Beauty, we all agree, is skin deep at best.
What's underneath is all that really counts
And all that glitters isn't gold, except on
Social media where what you see is all you get,

And when the skin begins to sag, we gasp,
Renew, regenerate, replace, revive
The epiderm with quackery, a salve,
A blade or clinging to a memory.

Although to be a duck's enough. To be
Content with all there is, to feel at ease,
within your skin, unafraid and mirror-safe,
To not regret not growing up to be a swan.

Illumination

The men who came to build the concrete walls,
The giant dams that stopped the rivers' flow,
Made reservoirs of energy on hold until
A switch was thrown and spinning turbines fed
By water down long slippery slides, could flood
The night, the prime domain of sleep, with light.
The power of the sun, the water, height
And gravity, the toil of flesh and blood,
The science, engineering nous, the dead
Whose bones lie underneath the man-made lake
Have taken more than rain and tears to fill.
The cost of making super waterfalls
Was losing time for dreams but who could know
The quest for light might be our worst mistake.

Flooding the Black River

There was a time when the river
Was no more than a line of pools,
Puddles connected by potential
Rather than by an actual flow.

The riverbed was dry as old skin,
And any living thing that could,
Lay dormant, dried out or died
Despite the certainty that this place

So verdant, so water-rich, so cold
Could never be laid bare by drought.
Not for long, not for real, surely not,
Not with snow atop the mountain peaks.

But I have sat on that timber bridge
Tossing pebbles into the dust,
Watching little lizards scatter about,
While costing feed to be bought in town.

This last week though, there's been
More water coming down the banks
Than they can hold, and the bridge
Is underwater and the skinks are wet.

Camera crews circle overhead
Because the visceral spectacle
Of cattle as they die makes for
Better footage than bleached white bones

Especially from overhead, it seems.
Hired four-wheel drives have
Brought up shaking-headed disbelief,
Superficial sympathy, and questions

That demand a twenty-second answer
To a problem that took climate change,
Governments and God years to form.
A soundbite to accentuate the news.

I'll pass and leave it to my eldest son
His wife, a local girl, and both of his kids.
They know how to do that stuff.
They've had enough practice now.

I'll watch them tonight on the telly
Stoically saying the river's in flood
And our livelihood's at risk.
Maybe someone could start an appeal.

Now there's a break in the weather
I'll go and look at the damage,
See if there's anything useful to do
Upstream, always the start of it all.

There are cows on the other side
Of the river, more like a lake,
Friesians up to their udders in mud.
It might need the tractor. If not,

They're hardly worth slaughtering.
They're milkers not beef. Anyway,
Even in good years we almost pay
Buyers rather than them paying us

For the milk, and they flood the market,
The shoppers don't care. Milk
Comes from cartons rather than cows,
I think there's some rope in the shed.

The Inglis

The River Inglis runs unmanicured
From sky to shore. The Campbell Ranges tease
The clouds until they burst, the water fall
Creating little rills and becks that seek
Each other's company to form the streams
That flow into a single word. No doubt
There was an older name or toponym
But no one knows, the river least of all.

It runs from somewhere nearby Hanson's Peak
And dances down towards the coast without
Intelligent design. No plan foresees
Such artless curlicues, it is the free
Calligraphy of nature's wildest dreams.
Its unpredictability ensured
Its course remains undammed. A trout can swim
Upstream without a bar, then back to sea.

The Last Yeoman of the Leven River

The flood plains of the Leven River
Are fertile, black and often submerged.
You take your chances. A good year
Brings a bumper crop, money in the bank
Enough you hope, to last through the years
When the river refuses to stay in its banks,
When everything's sodden, when the chance
Of some profit is sluiced down to the sea.
Every field sown, every crop planted
On Gunns Plains is a gamble, every time.

Billy Last could turn a furrow
As straight as a die, manhandling
A single blade plough behind his horse
Even as a tractor gathered dust
In his shed. Billy liked to feel the soil,
Smell it as it rippled and broke like a wave.
On a tractor, you must turn on your seat,
To look back at a job that's already done.
Behind a good horse you make your own future
And Billy Last liked looking ahead.

Billy's dog is old and blind as a bat,
Now no more than a pet but part of the team
For as long as there is breath going in
And coming back out. Billy would laugh,
'Him blind and me who cannot see
More than five chain at best. What a pair!'
But a good dog's a good friend. Anyone who
Said it would be kinder to put him down
Should, in Billy's mind, never be let have a dog
And never be trusted as a dependable friend.

Billy'd never been to any school.
'Not for a day or an hour or a minute,'
He'd say without a hint of romance or guilt.
'More's the pity.' But he'd learnt to sign
His name on a cheque even though he
Couldn't write the amount that he'd pay.
'Just fill her in yourself,' he'd say.
Billy believed a man's word was his bond
And no one on up here needed to thieve.
If you were caught short, you just had to ask.

But Billy kept a ledger in his head with lines
As straight and neat as the furrows he ploughed.
From well before sunup he worked until dusk
'Til every red line was black and nothing was owed.
For a man without letters and precious few words
Everyone knew that his numbers were right.
You earned what you could, turned pennies around
And the pounds would look after themselves.
After his funeral, when they read out the will
His children applauded the sum of the man.

Trout Fishing on the Blythe

If I must hypothesise,
I'd claim that any place
Where trout swim wild
Is beautiful without
Exception or debate
Although I acknowledge
The limits of my claim.

Maybe then, I'd speculate
That to fish in flowing rivers
Just lets me be alone
Because the limitations
Of anybody's claim
Are of no concern to the trout
That swim past the lures.

So if I must now theorise
I'll say no more than fishing
In a creek that isn't named
And therefore not betrayed
By any map, will never be
A waste of quietude
Or patience (tested again).

As the dawn's rising light
Turns water to gold, before
The mountains around you
Have colour, while birds still
Call hopefully urgent and
The breeze is still cool, you wave
And cast out a fine line.

The light disappears.
After you've sent a handful
Of parrs downstream with whispered
Instructions to grow fat and return,
After you've lost a fish that
Tore itself off so near to the surface
You could smell it,

Then, if you're lucky
a nibble, a feather that
Gains weight and after you reel
In excitement to land it, you
call it a day, for one is enough.
With your bag in your basket
You head off for home.

It's not until long after
You've slid a net under
A table-sized fish that you'll see
Such light again. It squirms
In the back of your ute,
Around every corner until
The road becomes sealed.

At home in the laundry,
you gut it, wrap entrails in old news
And scrape at the skin.
If the light is just so, it
Reignites rainbows in
Every fish scale and brings
Back the river at dawn.

The Last Duchess

It is a stencil on a slab of stone
A little hand outlined by ochre blown
From someone's mouth, a spray of clay and spit
That left behind a perfect print of it
Upon the ceiling of the cave. Who knows
The reasons for such art but now it shows
How real she was, a memory here enveiled,
And under my control. You'll note I've styled
It as a proper painting even though
It is a childish thing. And do you know
The russet clay came from quite nearby here,
From underneath the river. When it's clear
It shimmers like pool of flowing blood.
They seem to prize the stuff, a special mud.
The men, if such they are, will rub it in
Their matted hair or smear it on their skin,
Parading 'round as if they own the place!
You doubt my word, I see it in your face,
But it is true. The ones who still remain
Refuse to yield to God in my domain.
It may amuse to hear the circumstance,
The little tale behind its provenance.
I'd been out hunting with dog and gun
Some morning sport beneath a gentle sun
When walking on the river's bank I heard
A sound and thinking it may be a bird
I raised my piece to see within my sight
A native girl, there struck dumb by fright.

I'd caught her unexpectedly, alone
A naked forest nymph, near fully grown
She dashed away and were it not for Pup
She may have got away. I found her up
The riverbank, beneath a stony canopy
Where she lay still as I relieved my need.
The moment I relaxed my grip, she ran
As if I meant her harm. What kind of man
Did she assume I was? I'd offer her
A chance to live. I see your doubt but sir
It is the truth. In any case, she fled
I gave no chase for up above my head
An audience of hands appeared to wave
A wondrous sight I'll carry to my grave.
So, I, determined to acquire a hand
Or two, mementos you will understand,
returned with tools and chiselled out the one
You see before you here. The damage done
To other prints was quite severe; the heft
Of hammer blows destroyed more than it left.
I'm not entirely sure the hand is hers
Of course, but nonetheless it serves
Another purpose now, reminding me
I'd let her go, a sign of sympathy,
For though I am a Curr by name, you'll see
I always work through God and God through me.

So, when I gave the shepherds leave to sport,
To hunt the mob of blacks nearby, I thought
She would have warned the tribe or left to save
Herself, but she preferred the common grave
With others of her kind. Or it may be
That she succumbed to earlier wounds received
But no one now can say what did occur.
Or what indeed could have become of her.
The men dispatched the wounded and the dead
Down cliffs into the sea and turned it red,
An overused description, yes I know
But those who saw say it was really so.
And over there some other souvenirs;
A skull, a scrotum pouch, a pair of ears
A stone they used to grind their precious cream,
Mementos of a near forgotten dream.
The bell! We'll go together down to dine.
The cook has roasted lamb and I have wine
From France, an earthy nose and then a song
Perhaps. Or an early night; we're still a long
And painful distance from the civil world.
While on our way note Glover's work, good sir
The artist is a master, yet I prefer
A less romantic view of those he paints.
He turns the sinners into Rousseau's saints.

Wild Rivers

The Franklin runs from cradle to the sea
Through corridors of ancient wilderness,
A habitat both uncontrolled and caged
As if the river were a snake as claimed,
And all that's left of all that was at stake.

In the time when nothing was corseted,
When water flowed through self-made
Chasms, un-engineered by human hands,
Before its course was named and mapped,
Before it turned into a photo opportunity,

Before it was a challenge to the brave and fit
And well-insured for whom it comes
With rescue crews and helipads,
Or volunteers to find your bones.
When that is all the river gives you back,

When the meaning of the river was as wild
As the river was itself, when no one was there
To say that it was, when no change to the flow
was made by the seeing or naming it, once
or twice, then it was wild, then it was free.

My neck, my arms and legs, any flesh
Exposed, has been burnt, either by
The sun or wind, or a leech-death flame.
My feet have cooled on the river's bank.
This weekend wilderness exists for me.

Estuarine Flow

The flow that gouged a path through mountains fans
Into a broader view. The river's force
Has been reduced to rinsing lichened rocks
And swaying grass in mossy pools, benign
Enough to cool the heels of shoeless souls,
The riches brought downstream, alluvial dust
Of ages, have settled on the shallowed shore.

I know this habitat, the tidal gate
Between the sea and land, the soul's domain,
The liminal space between the here and gone,
The dissipated past dissolved into
The wider soul, returning to the source.
The river is the flow, the movement from
The source to sea, the journey and its end.

www.ingramcontent.com/pod-product-compliance
Lightning Source LLC
Chambersburg PA
CBHW072214070526
44585CB00015B/1327